Sick of It

Written by
Daisy Hawkins

Illustrated by
Caroline Garcia

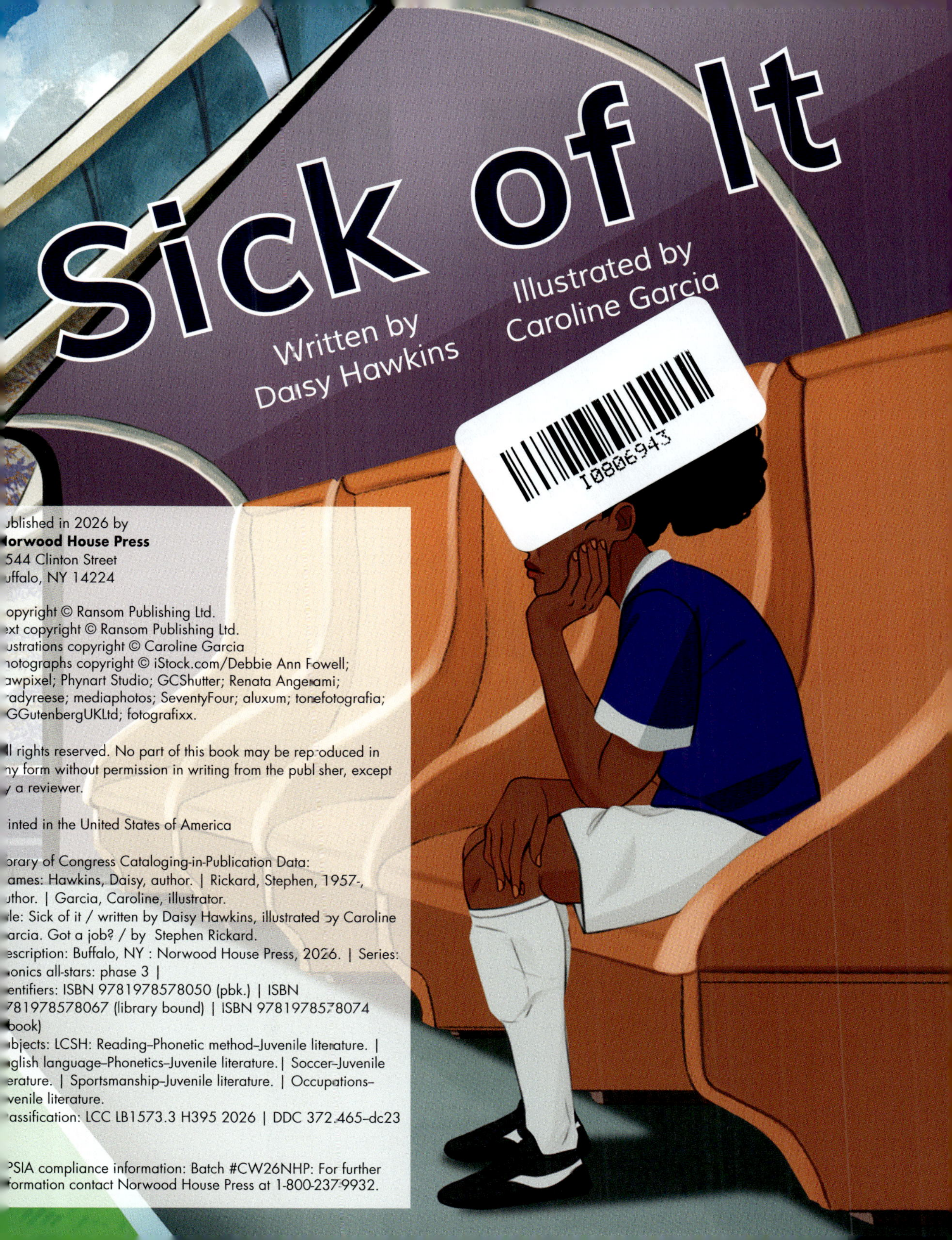

ublished in 2026 by
orwood House Press
544 Clinton Street
uffalo, NY 14224

inted in the United States of America

ibrary of Congress Cataloging-in-Publication Data:
ames: Hawkins, Daisy, author. | Rickard, Stephen, 1957-,
uthor. | Garcia, Caroline, illustrator.
le: Sick of it / written by Daisy Hawkins, illustrated by Caroline
arcia. Got a job? / by Stephen Rickard.
escription: Buffalo, NY : Norwood House Press, 2026. | Series:
onics all-stars: phase 3 |
entifiers: ISBN 9781978578050 (pbk.) | ISBN
781978578067 (library bound) | ISBN 9781978578074
book)
bjects: LCSH: Reading–Phonetic method–Juvenile literature. |
glish language–Phonetics–Juvenile literature. | Soccer–Juvenile
erature. | Sportsmanship–Juvenile literature. | Occupations–
venile literature.
assification: LCC LB1573.3 H395 2026 | DDC 372.465–dc23

PSIA compliance information: Batch #CW26NHP: For further
formation contact Norwood House Press at 1-800-237-9932.

Viv is in the Jets ...

... but Viv is a sub.

Viv is sick of it!

Viv is sick of it. She is wet.

I am wet and
fed up. I bet I will
not get a kick.

Viv is sick of it in the sun.

I am hot and fed up. It is not fun as a sub.
01

Viv gets a jab in the back.

It is the boss of the Jets!

Viv is not a sub!

Viv jogs on and gets to run. No fuss!

Viv gets to kick.

It is in the net! The Jets win!

A bit less sick of it, Viv?
Viv gets a big pat on the back.
01

Got a Job?

By Stephen Rickard

I got a job.

I will fix the tap.

I got a job.

I sell hot dogs in a box.

I got a job.

I can wax legs.

I got a job.

I can get the pills.

I got a job.

I can sell the jam.

I got a job.

I will fix the van.

I got a job.

I will sell a hat.

I got a job.

I sell wigs.

I got a job.

I am a vet.
I will fix
the pet.

I got a job.

I will jog.
I will huff, puff ... and win!

And me?
Did I get a job?
I got a job as well.